T0131936

Emmanuel's Barn

Medgeen Fabius

Copyright © 2022 Medgeen Fabius.

All rights reserved. No part of this book may be used or reproduced by any means, graphic, electronic, or mechanical, including photocopying, recording, taping or by any information storage retrieval system without the written permission of the author except in the case of brief quotations embodied in critical articles and reviews.

Archway Publishing books may be ordered through booksellers or by contacting:

Archway Publishing
1663 Liberty Drive
Bloomington, IN 47403
www.archwaypublishing.com
844-669-3957

Because of the dynamic nature of the Internet, any web addresses or links contained in this book may have changed since publication and may no longer be valid. The views expressed in this work are solely those of the author and do not necessarily reflect the views of the publisher, and the publisher hereby disclaims any responsibility for them.

Any people depicted in stock imagery provided by Getty Images are models, and such images are being used for illustrative purposes only.
Certain stock imagery © Getty Images.

Interior Image Credit: Medgeen Fabius

Scripture quotations are from the Holy Bible, King James Version (Authorized Version). First published in 1611. Quoted from the KJV Classic Reference Bible, Copyright © 1983 by The Zondervan Corporation. Used by permission. All rights reserved.

ISBN: 978-1-6657-2740-2 (sc)
ISBN: 978-1-6657-2739-6 (e)

Print information available on the last page.

Archway Publishing rev. date: 07/28/2022

For my mother, Marie Immacula
Lizenska Pierre, a loving teacher.

There was a house
It was a little house.
Inside that house
was a mouse. The
mouse was yellow
like honey.

There was a house. It was a little house. Inside that house was a cat. The cat was white like snow

There was a house. It was a little house. Inside that house was a dog. The dog was black like night.

There was a house. It was a little house. Inside that house was a sheep. The sheep was brown like chocolate.

7

There was a house. It was a little house Inside that house was a cow. The cow was gray like silver.

9

There was a house. It was a little house Inside that house was a chicken. The chicken's head was red like strawberry

There was a house a little house Inside that house came a little baby. This baby lin lln special job lad l

His job was to live
like you and me.
He never sinned.
He didn't do any
bad things. He
to be sinless.

sins away

It was in a little house like this that Jesus came to dwell with us. Rev. 3:20 "Behold, I stand at the door and knock If anyone hears my voice and opens the

door, I will come in to him...

16

He wants to come
into your house;
into your school,
into your sad
times;
into you good
times

The Bible tells us in Isaiah 7:14 Therefore the Lord himself shall give you a sign; Behold a virgin shall conceive and bear a son and shall call his name Emmanuel.

18

He's in us.
He's with us,
Right here, today,

He will be with you as you sit down for dinner.

He will be with you when you wash the dishes

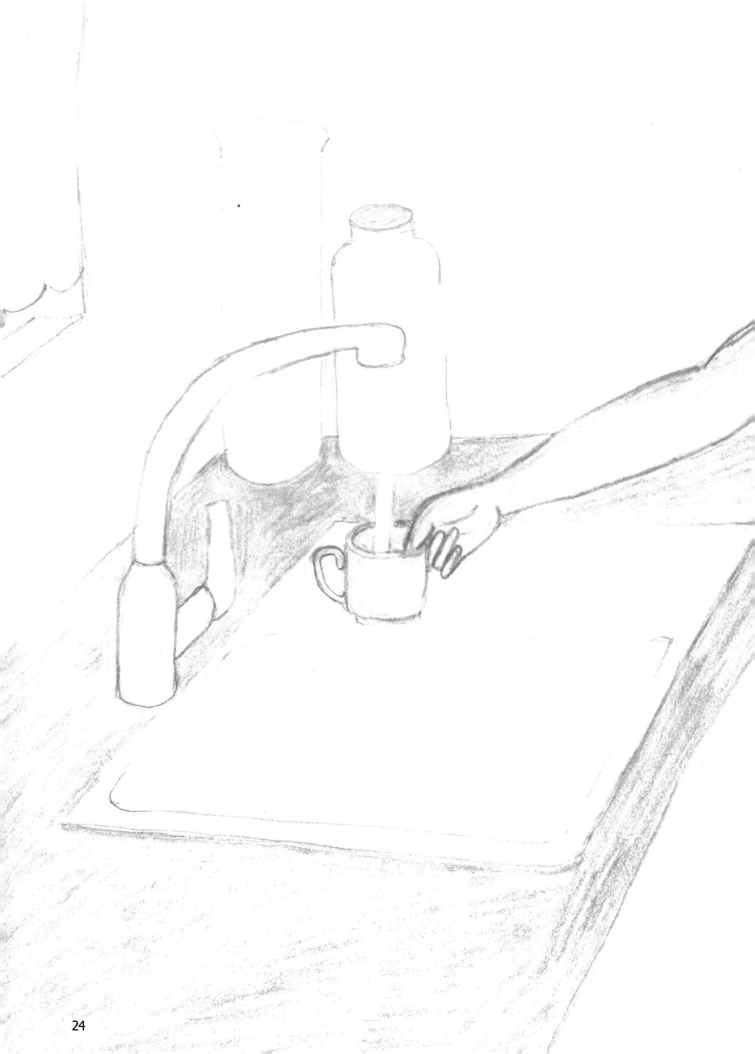

He will be with you when you visit your cousin from Boston.

God Loves yo

26

He will be with you when you are young. He will be with you when you are grown up. He will be with you forever.